# Simple Words Deep Thoughts

# By Joan Terwilliger

## ACKNOWLEDGEMENTS:

Thank you to Kelly Paradis, editor, and Alex Piacenza for all their work and experience, and for John Seaman who first inspired me to share my writings.

Thanks to Arizona Highways magazine for allowing me to take pieces from their beautiful pictures for some of the illustrations.

Thanks to J. Philip Newell books on Celtic spirituality that gives me a greater love for creation.

**ISBN:** 9798523599309
Published August 31, 2021

## AUTHOR'S NOTE:

I was born in Oakland, California but lived most of my life in southern California. I spent 20 years as a Sister of St. Joseph of Carondelet, teaching grade school and art. I graduated from Mount St. Mary's University with an art and history major.

I now live in Prescott, Arizona, with my roommate Carolyn Gonsalves, and our beautiful calico cat Talulah.
Both Carolyn and I are artists and love nature. Here we are, surrounded by loving friends and neighbors.

I hope these simple words bring you deep thoughts and peace.


Joan Terwilliger
August 2021

# CREATION SPEAKS

1. Love Of Creation
2. God Is All
3. Thin Veil
4. Oneness
5. Hidden
6. Holy Holy Holy
7. Earth – Mystery
8. Mother Earth
9. Light Life
10. A Grain
11. Flowing Light
12. Spirit Of Love
13. Winds Of Life
14. God Everywhere
15. You Are Within
16. Awareness
17. Nature World
18. Clouds
19. Stars
20. The Monsoons Are Here!
21. Living Air
22. Moisture
23. Cold To Glory
24. Faces Of Water
25. Dark Ocean
26. Water Spirit
27. Leaves
28. Blossoms Of Joy
29. Green Grass
30. Blessing
31. After Thoughts

# REFLECTIONS

33. Reflections
34. Love Everywhere
35. Reality
36. Deep Deep Thoughts
37. Darkness
38. Thoughts
39. Winged Prayer
40. Prayer
41. Remain In Me
42. Stop
43. Struggling To Rest
44. Desert – Life
45. Choices
46. Love's Vision
47. Weeds To Love
48. Root Bound
49. Moving On
50. Birds
51. Know You Love You
52. Flight Fear
53. Lost Found
54. Pride
55. Gone
56. The Way?
57. Change
58. My Cross
59. Imperfections
60. Lump To Glory
61. Rescued
62. Nemo's Tale
63. Downs And Ups
64. Fill Me
65. Life's Pieces
66. An Invitation
67. Baptism
68. Temples
69. Lights Of Love
70. Life Death Life
71. Heaven

72. Time
73. The Gift
74. The Note
75. Stained Glass
76. The Book
77. Family Of Love
78. Like Mother
79. Family One Body
80. Every Detail
81. The Service Master
82. Chair Lovers Foot Watchers
83. Christmas Lights
84. Joy
85. Eyes Of Faith

## LOVE OF CREATION

There is no plant in the ground
But tells of your beauty, O Christ,

There is no creature on earth

There is no life in the sea
But proclaims your goodness.

There is no bird on the wing

There is no star in the sky

There is nothing beneath the sun
But is full of your blessing.

Lighten my understanding
of your presence all around O Christ
Kindle my will
to be caring for Creation.


( An ancient Celtic prayer)

GOD IS ALL

Tiny or huge,
Big or small,
From the vast universe
To the atom so small,
To the beauty of a tiny gnat,s wing,
Or the stars numerous as the sands.
Or leaves clapping , grass swaying,
Ants scrambling, bees buzzing,
Humans pondering or bustling,
All are caught up in an universal
Symphony of love.
ALL IS GOD< GOD IS ALL!
And I am a part of it all!

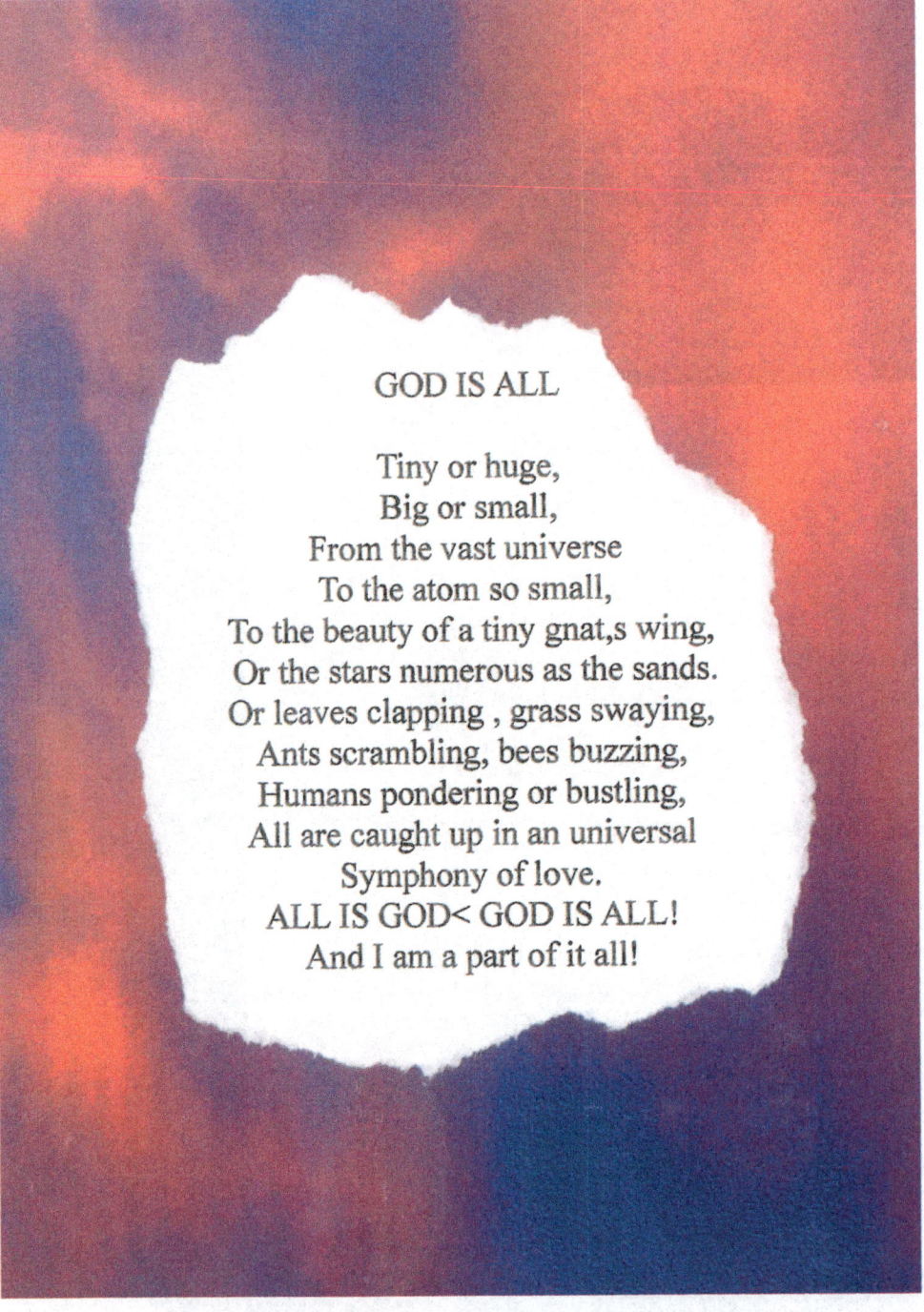

## THIN VEIL

The earth is full of your goodness.
(Ps.33)
Father God brought forth all creation.
Creation becomes God's child.
A thin veil separates earth and heaven.
God's light seeps through in creation,
and you are a part of it.
See it's goodness.
Christ was a veil piercer becoming light.
Saints are also veil piercers.
Lord grant me the grace
to be a veil piercer.
Falling in love with
the goodness of the earth.

## ONENESS

A deep red rose opening to a new day.
So casual a glance that caught the cosmic spark.
United in a surprise mystical instant!
We were together in love and oneness.
How can this be?
So different yet so one.

## HIDDEN

The desert was so hard, so rocky, so hot, so dry and dead!
Yet in the shade of a turned up rock
life in all its glory appeared!
There with its little translucent red face,
and warm green arms stood a small flower!
What a surprise! What a gift of love!
No one saw this little beauty, just me!
Oh, if only the whole world could see it!
In secret it grew, and if no one else saw it
it would still give Glory to God.
We are all called to witness.
Sometime we are called to bloom in secret.
Unseen actions, life, and beauty are everywhere
known only to our God of love.

## HOLY HOLY HOLY

Vast starry universe.
Mysterious three in one.
Creator and moving Spirit made flesh.
Holy Holy Holy!
The earth and all that it holds
cry out in praise!
O, little creatures rejoice
that you are living in this mystery.
For God has swallowed you up in its love.
That mystery three in one that
dwells within is our GOD of love.

# EARTH – MYSTERY

Earth's life is a mystery.

Life changes and moves
From mystery to knowledge.
Discovery is earth's life.
Seeking the why, where and when
Of the unknown.
As a child of God
Each of us is a Holy mystery
So to creature and creation.
With each breath and step
The unknown is known.
Listening silently brings peace
To mystery.

Earth's life is a mystery.
Eternity is knowing.

## MOTHER EARTH

Ground sandy black and brown.
Warm nurturing peaceful.
Water and light so very restful.
Humbly accepting being tossed in the air
landing home where awaits new birth.
The seed dark and warm changing in Mother Earth,
cracking, pushing out dark to light.
Thank you Mother Earth for your life.

## LIGHT LIFE

Under deep or shallow waters
Lies a magnificent world.
My spirit floats in and out with wonderment
And awe in this holy hidden world.
Saints and monsters
Dangerous or peaceful
Large and small.
Marvelous designs and color fits them all.
Whirling excited flashing fins
All caught up in a watery dance.
Joined by glorious multicolored moving plants.
In wonderment my soul is lifted high
To a creator so mighty yet so nigh.
This world would be lost without light.
Lost forever in the deep ocean night.
I humble thank you for your Divine light.
That shines in my dark night.

A GRAIN

I am a single grain on sand on the shores of eternity.
Not alone but joined by many.
As each snow flake is different so each grain of sand.
We are all unique in this community.
All united in love, service and beauty.

There are as many grains of sand on all the shores
of the world as there are stars in the sky.

# FLOWING LIGHT

God said,
 " Let there be light; and there was light."
                              (Genesis 1:3)
From command to reality!
Light brings warmth, healing, knowledge,
and life that flows like water
throughout all creation.
Small to great are drawn to the light.
From the moth frantically fluttering
around the light, to reptiles sunny for life,
plants silently, slowly moving to the light
for growth to cats seek light for
warmth and comfort.
All seek light, the heart of God.
Light flows like water throughout
all creation, and wants us to be a part of it.
Oh God, crack open this heart of stone
and let your light shine.
Let there be light and let it begin with me.
Breath in light
and exhale peace.

## SPIRIT OF LOVE

Burn in my heart that fire from above.
O Spirit of peace blow in as a dove.
Fill this vessel to overflow.
That I might be a yes and never a no.
Be that fire in my heart
so strong that we never part.
Let me be that spark of love
To witness that Divine fire from above.

## WINDS of LIFE

" You ride on the wings of wind."
                      (Psalm 104)
The wild swirling winds
swept over the new earth.
Bringing life. Moving life.
Tossing the light and dark
waters to the sky.
Tamed at times, but always
on the move.
A dome of time hovers
over all like a loving mother.
Separating the waters
of life and death, calming,
nurturing new life in God's
watery womb, seeding life
in the warm earth.
So much love!
Without fear blow with
God's Spirit wind.
Follow the love winds of Christ.
    Experience LIFE!

## YOU ARE WITHIN

You are above me O God.

You are beneath

You are in air

You are in earth

You are beside me

You are within,

O God of heaven,

you have made your home on earth
in the broken body of creation.

Kindle within me
a love for you in all things.


( An ancient Celtic prayer)

## AWARENESS

God is everywhere.
Lack of awareness does not
Make it less true.
With the silent spade
Of grace and humility
Pride and fear slowly fade.
Sparks of God's presence
Changes Life!
A new bigger world appears!
People and creation
Seen and heard anew!
All God!    All love!
Seek awareness!

## NATURE WORLD

Tall dark and mystic stood trees looking down on me.
My spirit is filled with unwanted fear and awe.
I am a stranger to this world loving it from afar.
Lord, teach me to love all your creation.
May the tall dark trees some day smile down on me.
Leading my spirit to hug them.

# CLOUDS

Clouds big and small of many shapes
Move slowly or run as in a race
Across the sea of blue.
Wind and clouds join together
Producing sky stories and music.
From to the rising  to the setting
clouds speak of the days to come.
Gray brings future storms.
Colors of nature brighten an
Excite their faces.
They are an introduction
to the heavens.
Could it be angles sit on them
And gaze down on us?

## STARS

Twinkle
Twinkle little star!
Oh, stars so bright.
Shine in the night.
Covered by day,
Darkness brings
sunlit stars to birth.
As numerous as all
Shores sands, yet each
Is called by name.
Some say that stars
are the souls of the passed.
Do you have a star?
You are called by name.
So for now, and for God
Twinkle!

## THE MONSOONS ARE HERE!

The monsoons are here!
Soon winds will blow.
Rain clouds will gather.
Lightening slices the clouds
and rain splashes and flows.
Then comes loud thunder, strong winds
and heavy rain!
All very exciting but dangerous.
In time the storm fades,
and all creatures arise to greet the stillness.
Dust gone. Trees and plants
glisten in the sun.
Birds flutter in small pools.
Worms falsely move to safety.
Death ends, but new life arrives
bring moist clean fresh hope.
Thank God, the monsoons are here!

## LIVING AIR

Wind gives voice to air
with moans, swishes and song.
Trees wrestle in the wind.
Pollen, seeds and dust fly to new homes.
Wind moves fire but also
introduced the fires of Pentecost.
Yes, the Spirit moves in the wind.
It moves with destruction and life.
Air is life!
Breathe in God's gift of air.
Air is universal  and so is the Spirit.

## MOISTURE

As I look down at
the dry useless sponge
my spirit can relate to it.
Sponges need moisture
to do the job of wiping,
washing, and cleaning.
Then from time to time
the master washes and
squeeze it clean.
Through prayer and silence
I am moistened.
With moisture I am willing to
be cleaned and to serve
over and over again.
My body maybe drying up
but my spirit is still moist.

## COLD TO GLORY

With cold, rain becomes white.
Cold white snow!
Cold white snow covering all.
Capturing sound and movement.
Turning shapes to white mounds.
Each unique flake silently falling
together creating a white blanket
that covers the sleeping earth.
One day the clouds separated
presenting blue sky and warm sun.
Melting the ghost like shapes.
Changing snow back to water.
Water glamour days were over.
Slowly trickling and running over
the imperfect ground awaking
seeds to new life of green and color.
Changing cold to glory!
May the dark cold, rain, snow and
waters of our life sprout new life
in God's warm light!
A new deeper life of love!

## FACES OF WATER

Life giving water with many faces.
Small joyful giggling streams.
Mighty waves clapping hands in praise.
Quiet meditative lakes
nurturing a secret life below.
Earth's life smiles in the rain.
Fog, Father God's life
silently moves covering all
in mystical gray changes
with the light of the Son,
Water, with many faces
most important to life.
Running to the lowest
seeks not to be the most important!

DARK OCEAN

Oh!
Deep dark, dignified ocean!
Gently nurtures below
 a fantasy world of
color and uniqueness.
From raging wild waves
to gentle swelling waters,
to running white surf
all a part of the deep dark ocean.
All proclaim God's life.

## WATER SPIRIT

Water, wonderful, wonderful, water!
cleanses, heals, quenches thirst,
and penetrates all creation.
Oh! thank you God!
Water so important
humbly seeks the lowest.
So too the Christ spirit.
Christ said, " Drink of me and
you will never thirst."
You are both water and spirit!
Drink daily of both waters.
Spiritual water is found in
creation, Scripture, silence and prayer.
Water, wonderful water!
Strengthen me, heal me, and renew me
in the springs of your love.

# LEAVES

Leaves,
the humble servants to the flower.
Giving, always giving!
Shelter, shade and food.
With the rhythm of the seasons
green turn to gold.
Then silently flouter to the ground
to run with the wind,
to surrender to a new life for all.
Leaves,
The teacher of life and death.
Signs of hope.

## BLOSSOMS OF JOY

Beautiful, beautiful, beautiful
wonderful, beautiful flowers!
My spirit sings for joy,
and dances in freedom!
Oh! Thank you God!
So many sizes, shapes,
colors, and designs.
Their Glory Crown!
Fragrance announces their presence,
saying, " I come to bring you joy."
In time and place all creation blooms.
In time and place you are called to bloom.
Fear not to bloom
Blossoms of joy!

P.S.  Stop to smell the roses.
    This will help you to bloom!

## GREEN GRASS

Green humble grass.
With water springs to life.
So many kinds,yet all the same.
Roaming freely the wild.
Tamed for useful beauty.
Restful to the eye.
Peaceful signs of life.
All enjoyed God's gift of green.
Ask to be green.
Let God's waters of life and love,
flow over you.
Spring forth peace, joy and love.
Be green for all!
Thank you God
for natures humble green grass.

BLESSING

May the grace of the love
of the stars be mine

May the grace of the love
of the winds be mine

May the grace of the love
of the waters be mine

I the name of the Word
of all life.

(An ancient Celtic prayer)

## AFTER THOUGHTS

Happenings and thoughts
Yesterday's shadows.
Thoughts renewed in the gray.
Some lost, some grasped at in the haze.
The Spirit moving and mending the wrong.
Secretly building the inner strong.
Nothing lost all part of today.
All a part of life to stay.

## LOVE EVERYWHERE

Love, love, oh, where is love?
Come to me!
Like cool water to the desert
Refreshing my dry desert heart.
Bright light to my confused twisted mind.
Mercy, mercy, mercy!
Forgive my restless impatient spirit.
Hope says, "All shall be well,
all shall be well."
Look up! Look up!
Step out of self-pity!
Humbly wait up the Lord.
Rejoice in all that God has done.
Receive God's love in all those near.
Stop fighting! Let go, let go!
Be at peace.

## REALITY

A fog a veil separates me from reality.
At the cross saints are afire with reality.
My heart sees and is left dual.
Break through this numb heart!
Only your Holy Spirit can do this.
Show me O' Spirit of reality!
Mean while I wait in the fog.
Could reality be heaven's surprise?

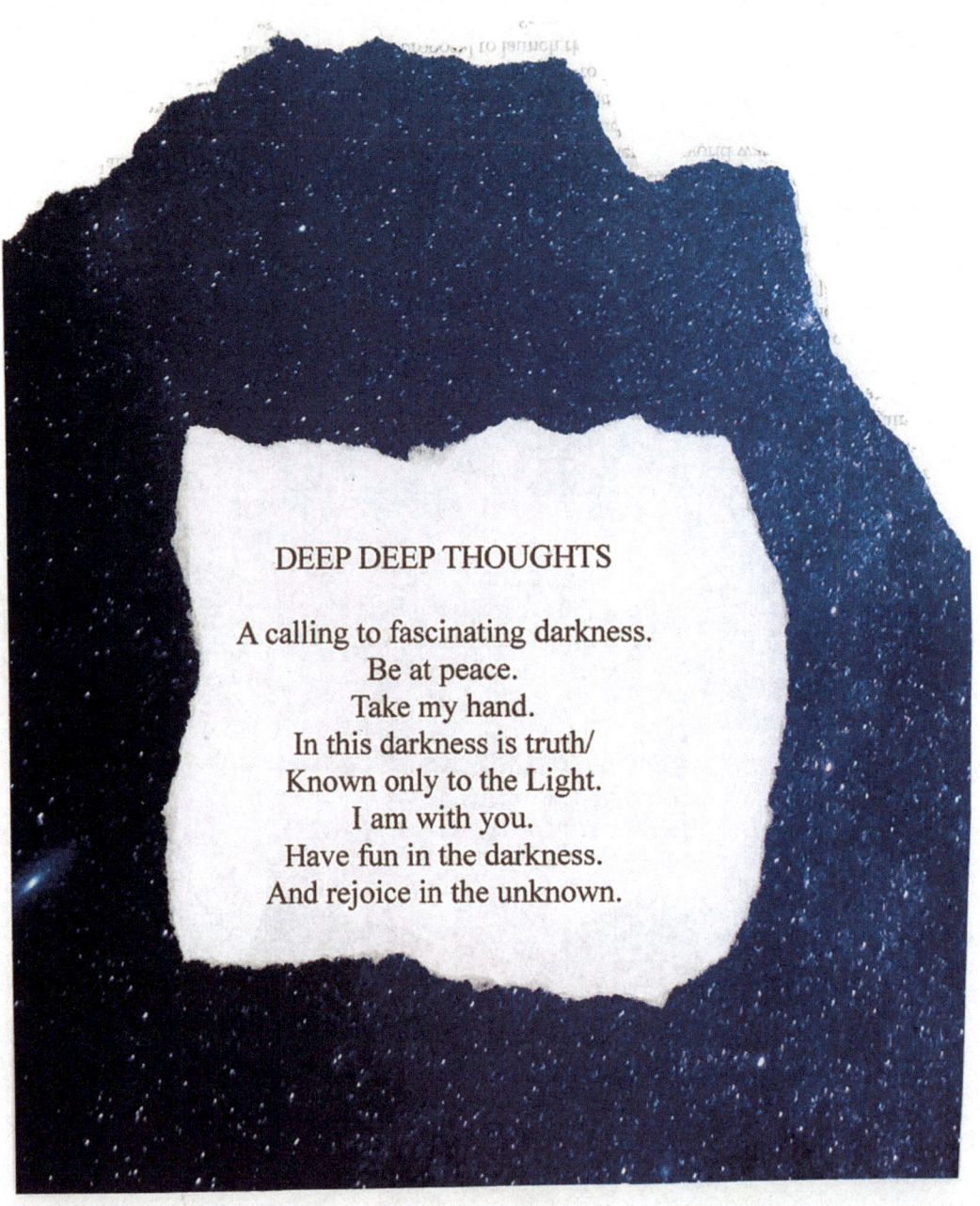

## DEEP DEEP THOUGHTS

A calling to fascinating darkness.
Be at peace.
Take my hand.
In this darkness is truth/
Known only to the Light.
I am with you.
Have fun in the darkness.
And rejoice in the unknown.

## DARKNESS

A call to fascinating darkness.
Be at peace.
In this dark darkness is truth.
Known only to the Light.
I am with you.
Take my hand.
Have fun in the darkness.
And rejoice in the darkness

## THOUGHTS

Wild wine are thoughts.
captured bring words to life,
creating thought pictures
and spelling stories.
Bring life and death.
Always on the move.
Wild wine thoughts
tamed and sobered  by love
brings thoughts and actions
of truth and beauty.

## WINGED PRAYER

Prayer of habit, discipline.
Prayer of mind, knowledge.
Prayer of the heart, miracles.
All prayer is a blessing.
Prayers are like winged love to God.
Listen deep!
Move from words to wordless prayer.
Stop!
Let your world catch up with you.
Silence knits happenings together.
Move with God's moving Spirit.
" Be still and know I am God."

## PRAYER

Prayer of habit, discipline.
Prayer of mind, knowledge.
Prayer of the heart, miracles.
All prayer is a blessing.
Prayers are like winged love to God.
Listen deep!
Move from words to wordless prayer.
Stop!
Let your world catch up with you.
Silence knits happenings together.
Move with God's moving Spirit.
" Be still and know I am God."

## REMAIN IN ME

" I am the vine, you are the branches,
Whoever remains in me and I in him
will bear much fruit, because without me
you can do nothing. ( John 15:5)

God's vine reaches deep
Into neutering earth.
Roots sucking up the waters
Of grace, shooting forth love
Branches high into earth's sky.
Branches free to choose
Life or death.
" Remain in me"
Yes, brings green leaves
Of service and rewards of fruit.
Time for pruning,
To bear more fruit,
Casting away the withered.
" Remain in me,
as I remain in you."

## STOP

Jungle, Jingle
Clitter, clatter goes the world
Flying high on ego gas into the unreal.
Flitting. Fluttering into a maze of darkness.
Whirling in circles of confusion and death.
STOP ! BE STILL!
And know you are not God.
Surrender to peace and silence.
Plant your feet down on the rock of truth and love,
and chose not death but life from above.

## STRUGGLING TO REST

Flitter, flutter, wandering
Goes my uncontrolled mind.
Wandering, restless searching
Here and there.
Sparks flitting and igniting old thought paths.
That float quietly and secretly in and out.
Round and around until discovered and put aside.
Breath in breath out. Ab-ba Ab-ba Ab-ba!
Put aside this battle and humbly rest in your
Human flutterings and allow your thoughts
To fall into the running stream of your weakness
And rejoice in the truth that God's love
Is made strong in weakness.

# DESERT - LIFE

Into the desert we go.
Into the desert we go.
Hi ho, hi ho! into the
desert I go!
Singing with self confidence
Until reality appears.
Oh!, It's so hot, so dry!
Where is the food, water?
And so many creepy crawlers!
With solitude I am face
To face with my creepy crawlers!
Lord, help me out of this place
Of suffering!
With God's waters of grace
And love's food comes life!
No way out but through
The door of hope and humility.
With a step from the sand to green
Comes a new song.
Into life we come!
Into life we come!
Hi, ho hi, ho! Into life
I come!

CHOICES

What star do I want to follow!
A wordly star?
A heavenly star?
Looking up into the dark
I see a tiny little star.
Hidden in the dark so very far!
In an instant I hear its call.
Fear not the dark I am Lord of all.
I trust you and I reach out for His hand.
O, Lord  lead me through this mystical land.
From the dark to the light.
Free me from fear in this night,
And secure me in your heavenly star light.

## LOVE'S VISION

"Lord, That I may see."
Cried the beggar in me!
So that I may walk right
In this spiritual night.
With Your mind and heart vision so clear
Wipe away my darkness that seems so near.
May our eyes be one in mind and heart
To see things as one and not apart.
For without Your light
There is no real sight.
Thanks for my many cracks within
Enabling Your love to come out and in.

## WEEDS TO LOVE

God said,
"That they all be one."
One humanity so many
people and differences!
Some good, some bad.
Some wheat some weeds.
Weeds being the universal divider.
Humbly accept your weeds.
With grace and time they fad.
Some stay till harvest time.
Measure others the same.
With unconditional and boundless love
I see God pulling up weeds and healing.
Remember!
Love covers a multitude of weeds.

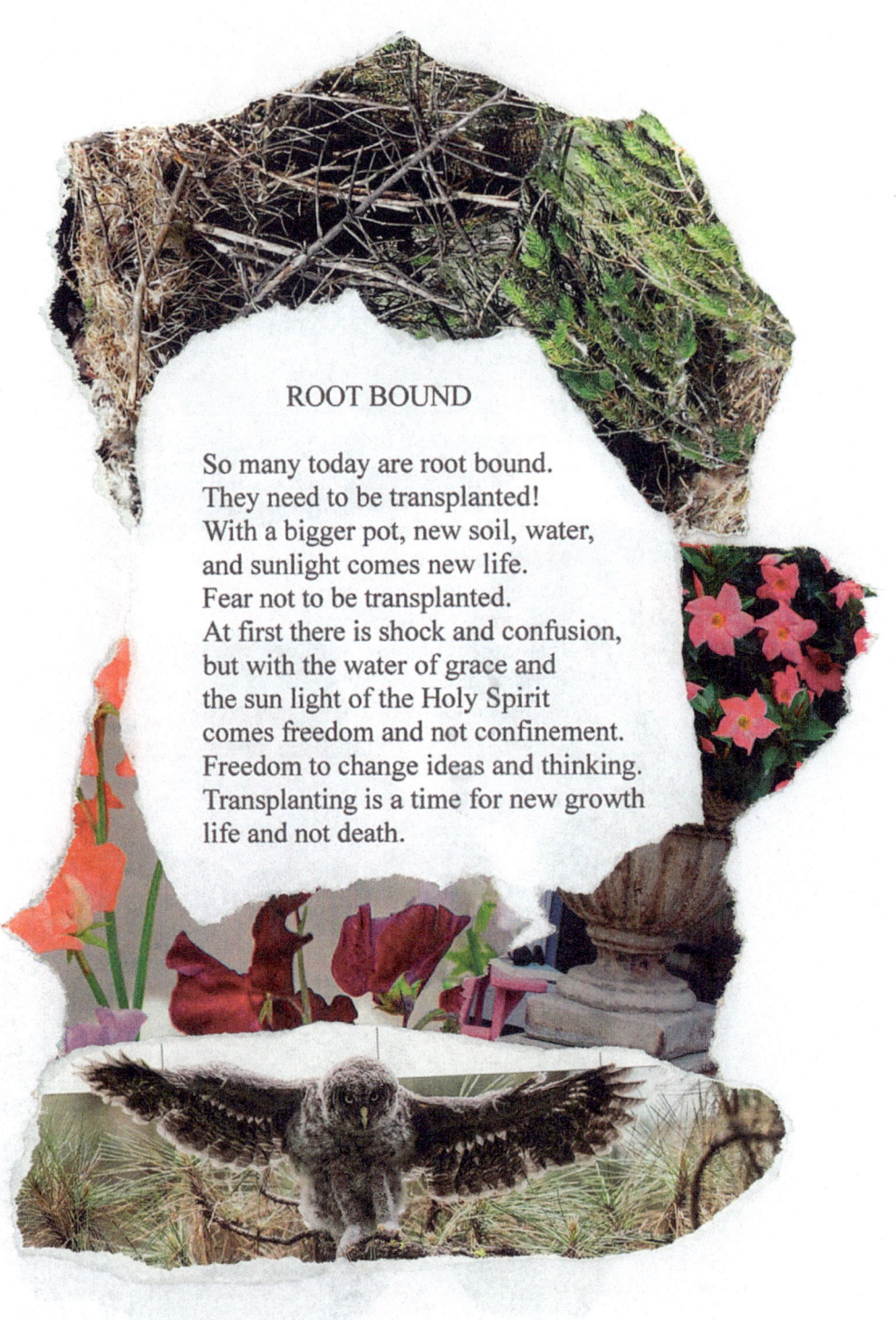

ROOT BOUND

So many today are root bound.
They need to be transplanted!
With a bigger pot, new soil, water,
and sunlight comes new life.
Fear not to be transplanted.
At first there is shock and confusion,
but with the water of grace and
the sun light of the Holy Spirit
comes freedom and not confinement.
Freedom to change ideas and thinking.
Transplanting is a time for new growth
life and not death.

## MOVING ON

Moving comes later or now.
Some are small some big.
 All in preparation for the big one - to Love.
Move from old to new,
from the known to the unknown,
to dark to light.
Let go move on – TRUST!
Move from life to death,
from death to life.
Move from earths cosmos
to time eternal.
FAITH says, All shall be well.
All matter of things shall be well.
Fear not!
Move on move on to LOVE!

BIRDS
Like a Humming bird
I flit from one thing to another.
Lord, give me
the strength and courage of the Eagle.
The intelligence and service of the Raven.
And the peace of the Dove, but
Thank you God for loving
 Humming birds.

You have searched me
and you know me, O, Lord
You know when I sit
and when I stand.
   (Ps 139. 1-2)

KNOW YOU LOVE YOU

Dwelling within me
You know me better
than I know me.
You see and know the
folds and creases of my heart.
All my faults and sins,
gifts and virtues.
The good and the bad.
You silently work
to bring me to completion.
No conditions needed.
Open wide to this free
merciful love that waits
patiently for your yeses.

I say yes my Lord,
I say yes, yes, yes!

## FLIGHT FEAR

I am like a small wiggly baby bird
with my mouth open wide
waiting to be feed and taken care of.
Do I really want to leave
this place of comfort and security?
Do I have wings?
Lord, teach me to fly.
With your support fear turns into trust.
Yes you can. Yes you can!
I can fly above the clouds
and with the blue of the wind
newness of life appears.
Thank you Lord for the strength
to move beyond the broken shell
to the freedom of a new birth.

## LOST FOUND

I am so wild and woolly.
This life I Fling to the sky!
Fears and doubts in my life
Pierce me deeply like a knife.
Who am I so young?
So wild and woolly?
Can my life be shared?
The deadly crash came so fast.
That life flung to the sky has passed.
No more doubts no more fears.
Who am I?
I know now for God is here!

# PRIDE

Standing high and looking down.
I am up, they are down.
I am right, they are wrong.
Standing high and flying
With birds of the feather,
Saying to myself,
What pleasure! what power!
While sitting on my nest
Of trophies came from below
A sweet smell!
The sweet smell of humility.
That awakened my rotten stench!
"Come down and wash in the
Warm waters of love and life."
" Why? And give up being God?"
God said," Sorry, there is only
One God, and that isn't you!"
Pride is death to God's Spirit.
Come down, come down!
And celebrate God' waters
Of love and life

## GONE

Sickness leaves me gone.
My independence is gone.
It's a time of weakness, vulnerability,
and dependence, Oh yes, I am gone.
Are there lessons to be learned?
With the fire of sickness comes truth.
That healing comes with time and other hands.
We come heart to heart with others sufferings.
Sickness gives me an appreciation for health.
Above all I am not God!
I become humbly gone in God.

### THE WAY?
There are so many ways.
Which way? A crossroad!
Which way?
I suffer in darkness and confusion.
Pray and wait in hope.  Pray and wait in faith and wait in love.
Then one day the darkens and confusion disappeared.
In the light the birth to the way was born!
In peace I walk.

## CHANGE

From time to time
a plant grows out of it's pot.
It needs to be transplanted.
Life changes continually.
It's a shock at first,
but with love and water
it's moved to a larger pot.
Without the change it would die.
The plant may experience
many new pots,
but eventually it's planted in
the garden with many other
unpotted plants.
There they grow in the sunlight
of love and peace.
CHANGE!
Let not fear, doubt, confussion
or guilt deter you,but walk
in faith and trust.
Change is life!
Listen and watch carefully
nature has many stories to tell.

## MY CROSS

"Pick up your cross and follow Me."
(Mt. 16:24)

All have a cross.
Oh, God, my cross is too heavy!
At nights dream,
I saw a dark endless hall.
Leaning on the walls
were crosses big and small.
Choose a new cross!
So many! Big one no! Not too small.
There it is!
Picking and turning over.
Surprise! My name, my cross!
Thanks, Help me God.
Teach me its lessons.
Join your crosses with Christ's
Pick it up and follow Him
to resurrection!

## IMPERFECTIONS

God said,"It is good."
But creation is full of imperfections.
God says, "It is good."
All are born imperfect,
Physically, emotionally, or sexually.
The Church and the world say, "Be holy, be perfect."
The ego says, " Work hard, you can do it."
God says, " Surrender, wait, I am at work.
My love and perfection has the ability
to include what seems imperfect.
They are part of my plan."
Imperfections lead to knowledge.
It's a chronic human condition.
Life doesn't have to be perfect to be wonderful.
Be at peace, laugh at your self you are ok!
Accept the ok and pass it on,
and stop making others perfect!
I walk straight with crooked lines.

## LUMP TO GLORY

A lump of clay was chosen by the potter
and thrown on the wheel of love.
With graces water and strong hands
the clay begins to move.
In the beginning the clay
yells and screams, but in time
it surrenders.
Slowly God begins to form a new creation.
When finished it's set out to dry
in the silent desert sun.
Then fired in oven of trials
covered with the robe of glaze
and fired again in God's love.
At LAST,
the beautiful shinny vessel
stands full of love and ready to be poured out!
Transformation from lump to Glory
comes with your yes.

## RESCUED

While sailing in the vast Gulf waters
a tiny bobbing speck was sighted.
Drawing near crying loudly and
frantically paddling was a tiny kitten!
Shocked and surprised! How! What! Why!
A mystery miracle!
Lifted out, in hand, it lay wet, cold,
frightened and hungry, but ALIVE!
After water, food and warmth loud
purrs of thanks were heard.
God heard!
God hears and responds always to
our cries!

He was named Nemo.

Maggie Rogers spotted this kitten in the water three miles into the Gulf of Mexico while on a scalloping trip Saturday.

10-week-old was found in Homosassa Bay, checked by veterinarian, adopted.

**Associated Press**

ST. PETERSBURG — When Maggie Rogers spotted something bobbing in the water three miles into the Gulf of Mexico while on a scalloping trip with friends, she assumed it was a turtle, or a piece of sea kelp.

But as the boat got closer and slowed down, she found it was a tiny, apricot-colored kitten. Nine inches long and screaming at the top of its lungs, the cat was paddling furiously.

"We scooped him up and he sat on the boat with me for eight hours," said Rogers, who is the finance director at the Clearwater Marine Aquarium.

"He was exhausted and stressed," Rogers said. "His heart rate was high."

The boaters on the 17-foot Scout Current Drift did not know how the kitten arrived in the Homosassa Bay. There were at least 40 boats in the crowded area where he was found, they said.

On Tuesday, three days after he was found, a veterinarian said the 10-week-old, 1-pound kitten had worms, but was otherwise healthy.

He was adopted by Rogers' sister-in-law. — and named Nemo.

Homosassa Bay is about 45 miles northwest of Tampa.

## DOWNS AND UPS

Help me!
Lord, I am drowning in the sea
Of frustration, anger and self pity!
Leaving me weak and bewildered.
Lord, have mercy and draw me
Out of this cold black sea!
Bring me to the warm sandy
Beach of reality.
Let Your gentle Spirit dry me.
Your warm sun light of love
Give me strength and courage.
Relying not on my own strength
But Your power within.
Thank You for darkness.
In darkness truth is revealed.
With enlightenment brings
Humble knowledge.
Knowledge with grace
Brings change.
All part of life's journey.
With healing time downs become ups!

## FILL ME

Life be in my speech.

Truth in what I say.

The Love Christ Jesus gave
Be filling every heart for me.

The Love Christ Jrsus gave
Be filling me for everyone.

( An ancient Celtic prayer)

## LIFE'S PIECES

Each minute, hour and day
is a pieces of life's picture.
The Divine artist puts
each piece on life's canvas.
Day in day out God paints.
The picture grows with each
shape, color or shade.
"Lord, may I see my picture"?
"Sorry, not until you cross
this world to the next".
There my picture awaits
with all the other life pictures.
What a wonderful heavenly
ART SHOW!

## An Invitation

The Lord said,
"Behold I stand at the door and knock
if anyone hears my voice and opens the door
I will enter their house and dine." (Revelations 3: 20)
I hear you Lord!
But wait I must prepare!
Quickly I spread the table with
the cloth of compassion, decorated
it with creations flowers.
My labor and service is the main dish
served with the wine of gladness.
Closing with sweet love bread pudding.
Then the Lord said,
"Stop doing I said open not prepare!
Open to my voice and invite me
to dine with you in unity and friendship."
Yes Lord!
Come into a love feast and to a real Potluck!

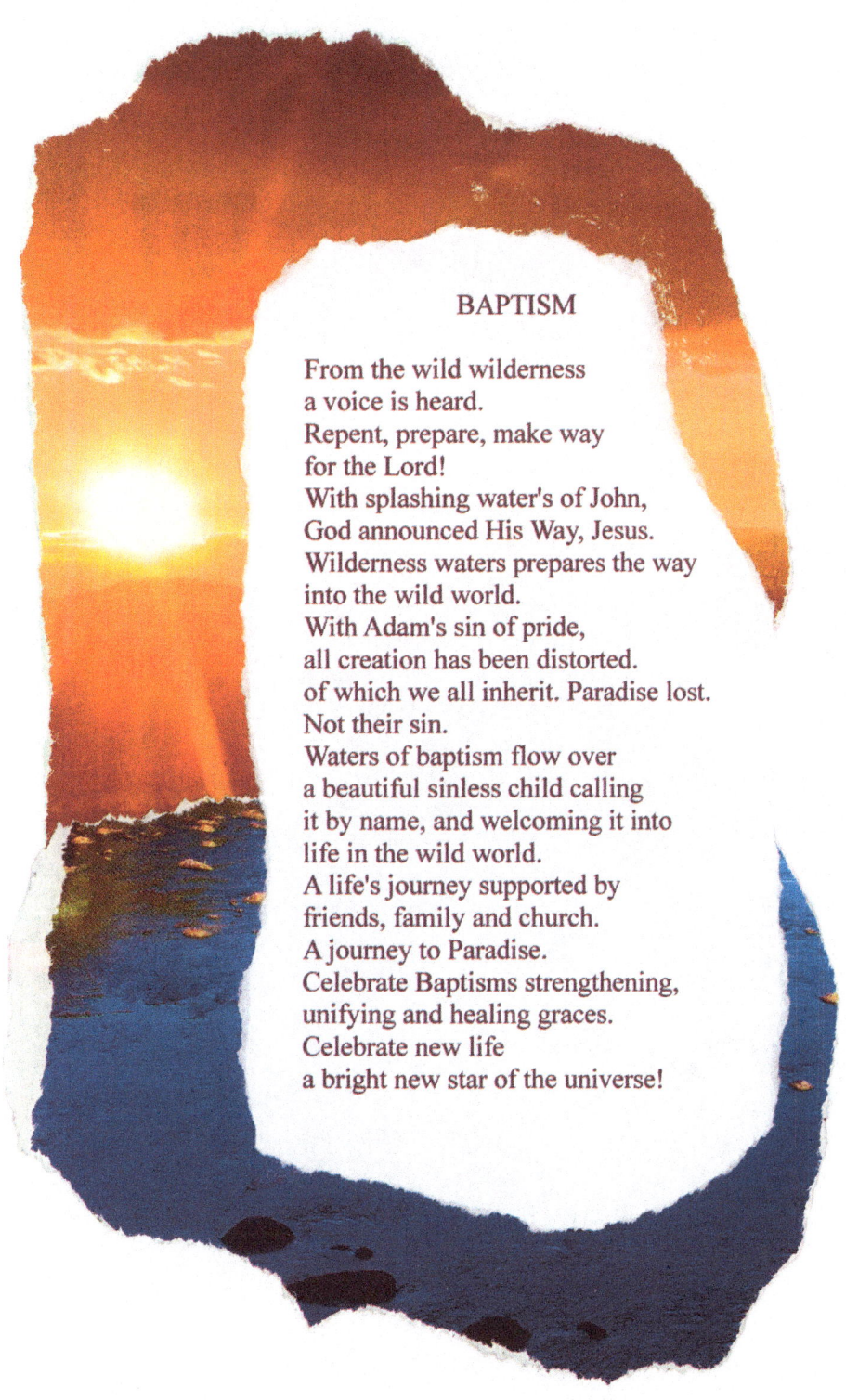

## BAPTISM

From the wild wilderness
a voice is heard.
Repent, prepare, make way
for the Lord!
With splashing water's of John,
God announced His Way, Jesus.
Wilderness waters prepares the way
into the wild world.
With Adam's sin of pride,
all creation has been distorted.
of which we all inherit. Paradise lost.
Not their sin.
Waters of baptism flow over
a beautiful sinless child calling
it by name, and welcoming it into
life in the wild world.
A life's journey supported by
friends, family and church.
A journey to Paradise.
Celebrate Baptisms strengthening,
unifying and healing graces.
Celebrate new life
a bright new star of the universe!

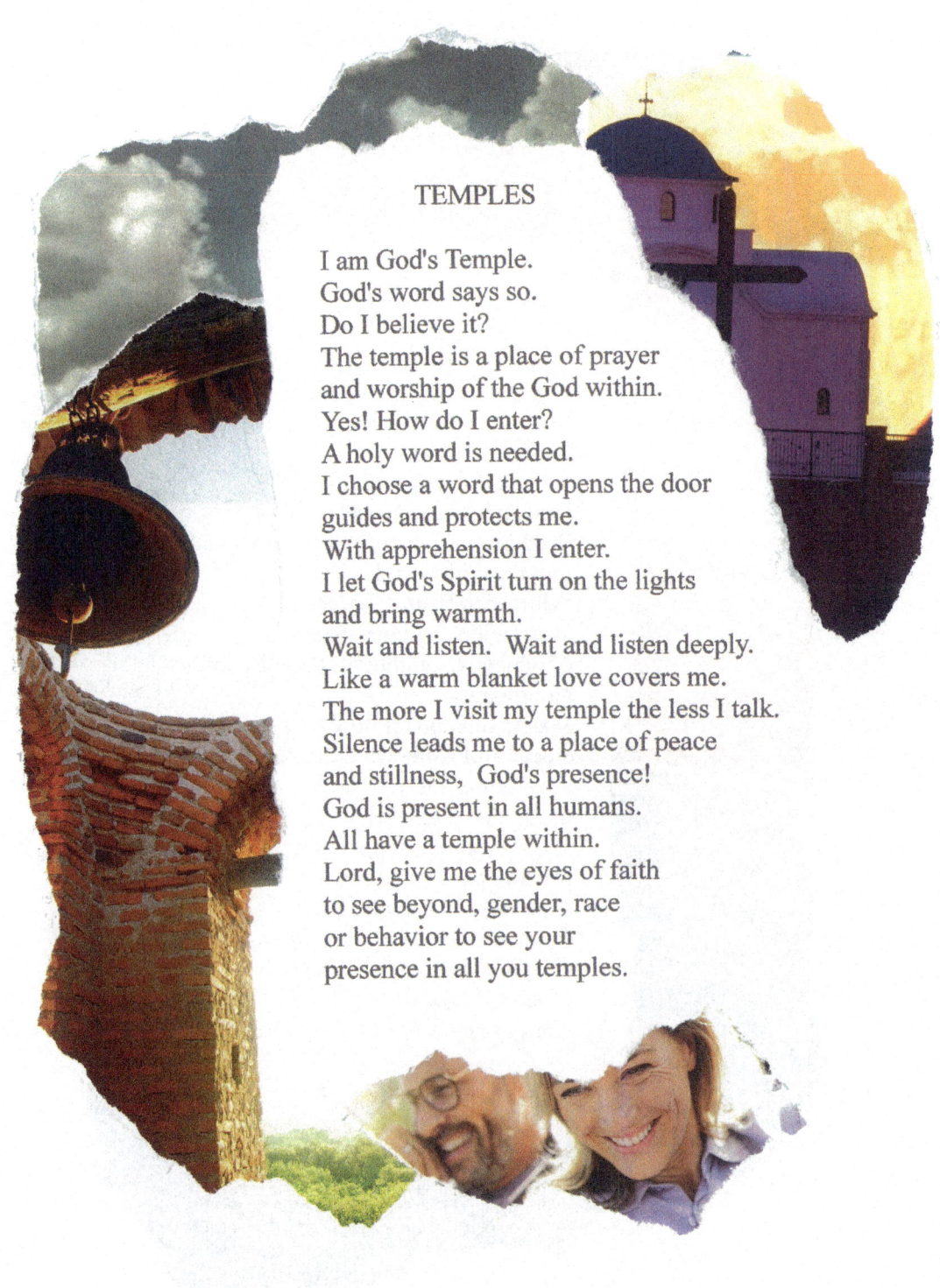

## TEMPLES

I am God's Temple.
God's word says so.
Do I believe it?
The temple is a place of prayer
and worship of the God within.
Yes! How do I enter?
A holy word is needed.
I choose a word that opens the door
guides and protects me.
With apprehension I enter.
I let God's Spirit turn on the lights
and bring warmth.
Wait and listen.  Wait and listen deeply.
Like a warm blanket love covers me.
The more I visit my temple the less I talk.
Silence leads me to a place of peace
and stillness,  God's presence!
God is present in all humans.
All have a temple within.
Lord, give me the eyes of faith
to see beyond, gender, race
or behavior to see your
presence in all you temples.

## LIGHTS OF LOVE

With the final surrender comes
the irresistible light of love,
Judging, rewarding, cleansing.
Blindness gone!
Freed from earth the true self
appears like a shining star.
Welcome home!
Uniting voices and presents
of God and loved ones,
enveloping me in rapturous love.
Welcome home to eternal
lights of love!

## LIFE DEATH LIFE

Time before time
I was born.
From warm womb
To cold world.
From first inhale
To last surrendered exhale
birthing continues.
Year in day out.
Life's journey unravels.
With the last thread
New life appears.
Freed from life's cocoon.
Freed from self love.
Free to fly to eternal love.
Time to eternity.
Life death life.

## HEAVEN

A bright light surrounds me.
I am drawn irresistibly to it source.
Fear falls, surrender leads from darkness to light.
No words or thoughts can explain only awe.
This light draws me deeper into a world of utter peace and joy.
There I am surrounded by my earthly loves.
It is a world of reunion and union
to all known and unknown.
No turning back!
All is irresistible love.
Home at last!

### TIME

Seasons move shadows
Days change lives,
and time ages.
The universe, world and all
of creation are on the move,
and cannot be stopped!
We are all children of time.
At birth we are given an expiration date.
Whether short of long time rules.
Not until we pass the black river
death will time surrender to
timeless eternity.

## THE GIFT

Thank you God for this day!
Each day is a gift.
A gift to be accepted in thanks.
After the bow of love
and the friendship wrapping paper
a surprise is revealed!
In the box appears more boxes!
Each of different sizes and color.
Each containing a love challenge
of joy, fear, anger, sadness.......
At the end of each day
with empty boxes and wrapping paper left
can we still say.
Thank you God for this day?

## THE NOTE

Sing praise to God! Sing praise!

We all have a note to play

and each note is important.

All creation also has a note to play.

Each note creating a sound of love.

All these notes fill the whole universe

with a gigantic sympathy of praise.

## STAINED GLASS

Light streaming throuh colored glass
Recapturing space invaded by darkness.
Light bringing to birth, something new.
Changing the ordinary to a circus of fun.
Magical delightful colored glass touches hearts
opening it up to thoughts above.
Rainbows – Hope – God – Love

## THE BOOK

Life is like a book.
There are many chapters
each chapter holding many pages.
As years go by chapters are finished.
Doors are closed and opened to a new chapter.
At the last chapter the book is closed.
But a new book appears.
God's book.
God's book of life
where many names are written.
I look closely. Yes, my name is written there!
Yes, in the book life without chapters!

# FAMILY OF LOVE

"The Father and I are one."
John 14:11

Two loves
Birthing love
Creats a family of three.
Father God creator.
Son Jesus enlightener.
Their Spirit breathing
life and power.
Bringing beauty, joy and color
To a dark world.
This bow of life, love and peace
Dwells with in YOU!
Oh! Spirit enlighten me
To this true reality!.
Tear away this veil of dakness.
May I with faith's eyes
see and live
With this family of love,
Becoming love.

## LIKE MOTHER

A seed freed from its nurturing mother
Fell to the ground.
Rain and wind covered it with earth.
Moisture brought change.
From its cracked shell
Tiny arms appeared, roots!
Multiplying and anchoring
This small life.
Above appears a sprout.
A stem, leaves, then flowers!
Just like its mother.
As a child of Mother God
I am called to grow, bloom
and spread life,
Just like my Mother.

### FAMILY ONE BODY

As I gaze at the picture of my past relatives
I see physical resemblance.
People say, " You have your Mother's nose,
your Father's mouth and your Grandmother' legs."
We are all part of the past.
I thank God for the people mixture
that makes me who I am.
With the good and bad god's grace can
transform them into His likeness.
For we all have God's DNA.
May the past be a part of today.
I am my own person, but a part of a family.

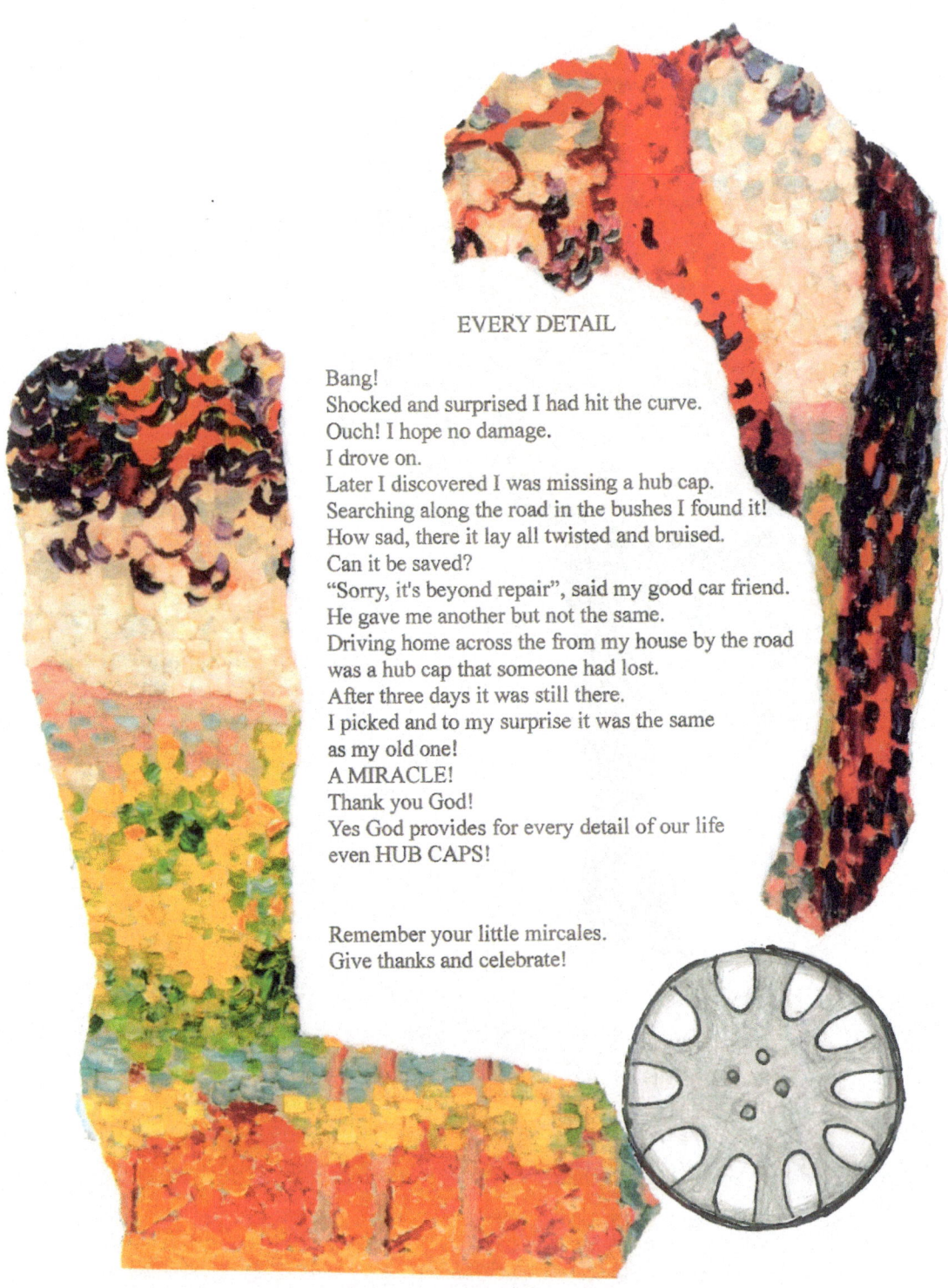

## EVERY DETAIL

Bang!
Shocked and surprised I had hit the curve.
Ouch! I hope no damage.
I drove on.
Later I discovered I was missing a hub cap.
Searching along the road in the bushes I found it!
How sad, there it lay all twisted and bruised.
Can it be saved?
"Sorry, it's beyond repair", said my good car friend.
He gave me another but not the same.
Driving home across the from my house by the road
was a hub cap that someone had lost.
After three days it was still there.
I picked and to my surprise it was the same
as my old one!
A MIRACLE!
Thank you God!
Yes God provides for every detail of our life
even HUB CAPS!


Remember your little mircales.
Give thanks and celebrate!

### The Service Master

By prayer we come to know
our Divine Service Master
that charges our battery with
strength and power, fills our
tank with over flowing love, and
wipes clean eyes to see inner
and outward truth, tunes up our
mind with knowledge and wisdom,
polishes our lips to speak words
of life and praise.
Oh yes! Thanks for the GPS
that keeps me on the right road.
The road with many ups and downs,
bumps and break downs, but the
Service Master is always near to help.
The road maybe long or short,
but it does end at the Master's door
where our old vehicle is exchanged
for a new one, maintenance free.
Start today! Get in touch with your
best service Master, GOD.

## CHAIR LOVERS AND FOOT WATCHERS

Change comes
with the accumulation of years.
Imbalance, dizziness makes cracks,
Edges and stairs enemies.
We become foot watchers.
With tired weakness, and pain
we become chair lovers.
We are all captives of age and time.
No stopping either!
We all one day must surrender
the body to free the soul.
But for now,
I am a chair lover and a foot watcher!

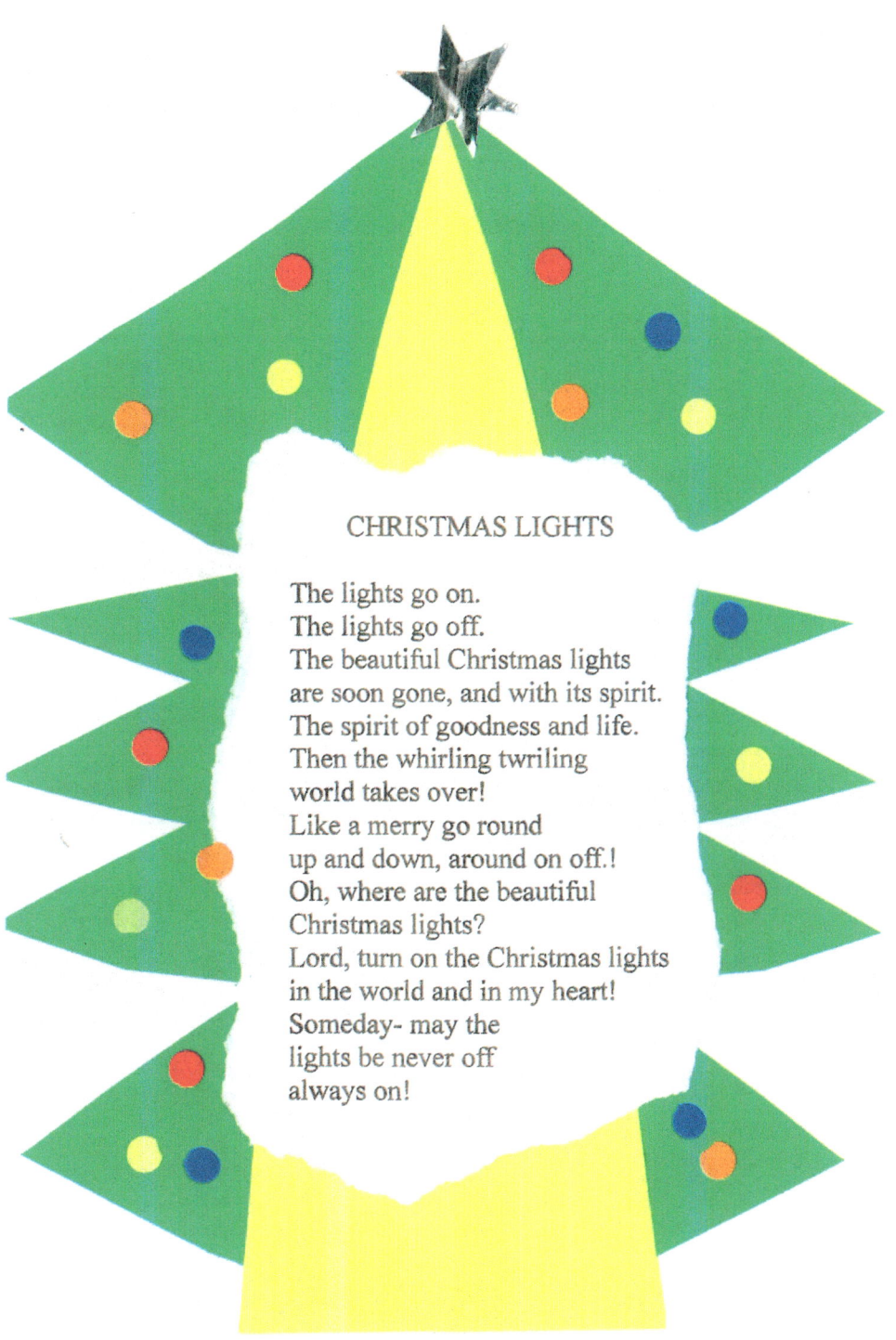

## CHRISTMAS LIGHTS

The lights go on.
The lights go off.
The beautiful Christmas lights
are soon gone, and with its spirit.
The spirit of goodness and life.
Then the whirling twirling
world takes over!
Like a merry go round
up and down, around on off.!
Oh, where are the beautiful
Christmas lights?
Lord, turn on the Christmas lights
in the world and in my heart!
Someday- may the
lights be never off
always on!

# JOY

One night while looking out my window
I saw a wonderful happening !
RABBITS!
Yes, rabbits jumping , twisting high in the night air.
Running, chasing and playing with each other.
Little furies of love and joy!
BEAUTIFUL!

Streams sing while rivers leap and splash for joy.

Mountains and hills smile.

Birds swoop, sore and sing.

Trees bow, wave and clap their leaves.

Horse jump, bow, prance and whinny for joy.

Dogs lick, cats purr both roll over with joy and play.

All creation is a symphony of joy and jubilation!
God's word says, "Rejoice in the Lord always, and again Rejoice."
Holy joy is courage and strength.
Be joyful – Be strong!

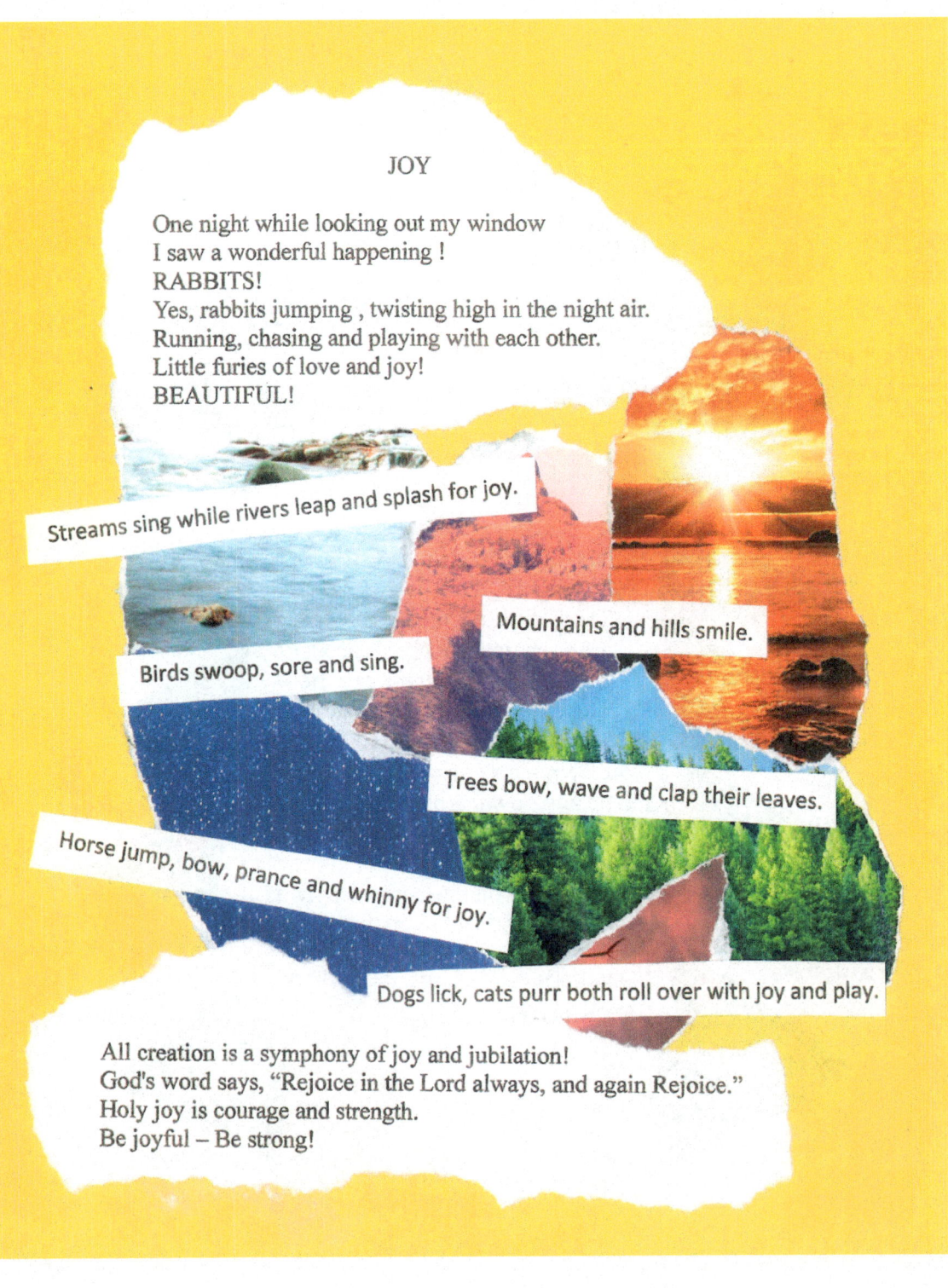

## EYES OF FAITH

Speaking deep thoughts
Were two young boys
Playing high in a tree.
" I won't believe in God
unless I can see Him."
The other in response.
" If you don't believe
you will not see God."
Reality follows faith.
With faith we see with
Difference eyes.
God's eyes.

(Out of the mouth of babes.
   A true story.)

Made in the USA
Columbia, SC
13 January 2022